MORE PEZ®
FOR COLLECTORS

MORE PEZ®
for Collectors

edition 2

With Expanded Price Guide

Richard Geary

Schiffer Publishing Ltd

4880 Lower Valley Rd. Atglen, PA 19310 USA

Dedication

In Loving Memory of: George, William and Marcia Geary, Debra Crowley, Lester "Butch" Burgett, and my Grandparents. They are dearly missed.

Library of Congress Cataloging-in-Publication Data

Geary, Richard.
More Pez for collectors / Richard Geary.
p. cm.
Includes index.
ISBN: 0-7643-0453-4 (pbk.)
1. Pez Candy Inc.--Collectibles--Catalogs. 2. Candy dispensers--
United States--Catalogs I. Title.
NK3690.G43   1995
338.7'664153--dc20   95-11069
CIP

Revised price guide: 1998
Copyright © 1995, 1998 by Richard Geary

Printed in China
ISBN: 0-7643-0453-4
1 2 3 4

Published by Schiffer Publishing Ltd.
4880 Lower Valley Road
Atglen, PA 19310
Phone: (610) 593-1777; Fax: (610) 593-2002
E-mail: schifferbk@aol.com
Please write for a free catalog.
This book may be purchased from the publisher.
Please include $3.95 for shipping.
Try your bookstore first.

We are interested in hearing from authors
with book ideas on related subjects.

Contents

Acknowledgments 6

Introduction 7

Chapter One
    Dispensers, Packaging and New Items 8

Chapter Two
    European Accessories 36

Chapter Three
    Candy and Displays 48

Chapter Four
    Premiums, Inserts and Conventions 58

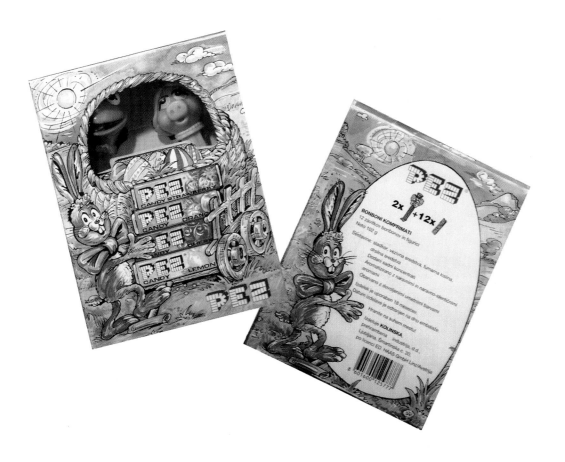

Acknowledgments

Thank you to Jim Kilgour, Lou Caldarola, Dream Castle®, Bill Clark, Chrissy Bailey, Doug Congdon-Martin, Rich & Sharon Davis, Eric Stransky, Ron Barr, and Rick & Michelle Plaga. A big Thanks to Steve Presser at BIG FUN (Cleveland, Ohio).

To Elaine, for the love and support in getting this project done. I love you.

Loving thanks to Jason, Bryan, Melissa, Matthew and Jacob, "The Geary Bunch," and to all my family, relatives and friends.

Introduction

So you want to be a PEZ® collector, but you don't know how to get started. Your first step should be getting all of the dispensers currently being made. Since there are newer models being introduced yearly and some characters being discontinued it is difficult to keep track of what is available. For more information you can contact: PEZ® CANDY INC., 35 PRINDLE HILL RD., ORANGE, CT 06477. It is important to note that the company does not carry older dispensers nor does it sell to the public. Your best sources for finding current dispensers is by going to local grocery stores, retail stores and most places that sell candy.

Finding older dispensers is becoming increasingly difficult, especially at lower prices. The hobby has been getting all kinds of media coverage, and this brings the value of several older models to the attention of the public. Still there are several avenues to finding older dispensers. The best success will be found at toy shows and in hobby publications. Dealers, however, are very aware of what they have, and experiences of finding bargains are far and few between. If you are willing to pay the price, your better dispensers can be found this way. The other, more obvious, ways to find dispensers are shopping yard sales and thrift stores, and by asking your friends.

It is difficult to establish the date of dispensers. After talking with a former employee, I think it is safe to say that not all dispensers came with the correct color base or patent number base.

How to display your collection is the most asked question. I have seen some very nice cases being made to hold dispensers, and I have seen some very creative means of presentation. What you do really depends on how much room you have to devote to your collection. Be careful though; if you stand them up by themselves you get the domino effect, when one falls over they all fall. Again, be creative and think about how you want it to look.

Chapter One
Dispensers, Packaging and New Items

The part of collecting PEZ® that is most fun is when new items are introduced. New items are coming out on a regular basis, and when they do, collectors always get excited. Several different PEZ® items are being made, such as watches, keychains, puzzles and more. Keep your eyes open, you never know when something new will pop up. A popular part of the hobby is collecting the blister packages, due to unique art work. Collectors often refer to items as M.O.C. (mint on card) and M.I.B. (mint in box or bag). Mint items in their original packages are considerable more valuable than loose items.

Revised Santa. The decal eyes now make this Santa come to life. $1-2

Revised Chick In Egg. Updated version of this Easter character. The egg shell is now a hard plastic (older version had a soft plastic shell. $1-2

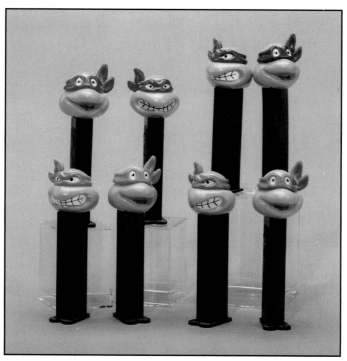

Ninja Turtles© Mirage Studios. Donatello (Purple), Leonardo (Blue), Michaelangelo (Orange) and Rafael (Red). $1-2

I-Saur™. New dispenser from the Pez®-A-Saurs™ series.
$1-2

He-Saur™. From the new Pez®-A-Saurs™ series. $1-2

e-Saur™. The new Pez®-A-Saur™ characters. $1-2

Fly-Saur™. New dispenser from the series Pez®-A-Saurs™. $1-2

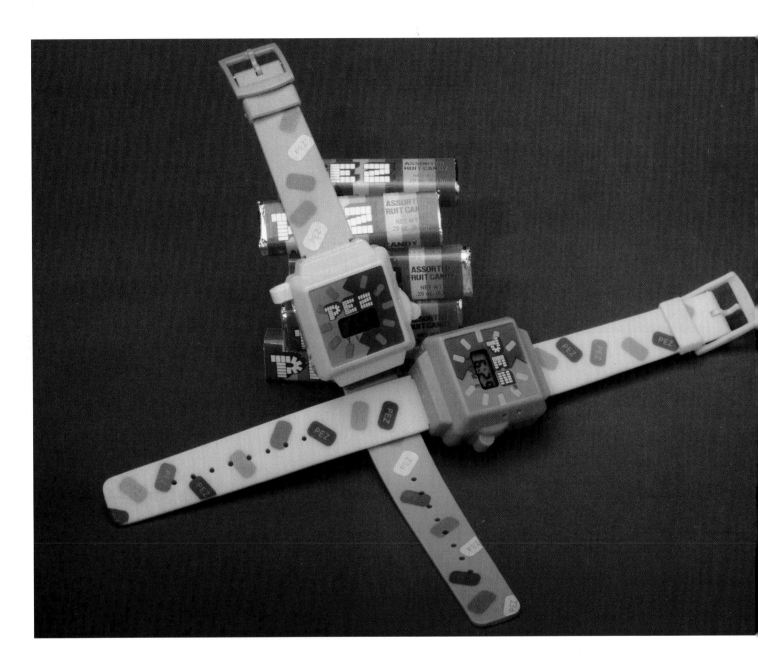

Pez® Watch. Made by Dream Castle™. This unique
item is the first in a line of products that would change
the way we remember the character dispensers. And,
yes it tells time and works as a dispenser. $10-15.

Pez® Watch. Made by Dream Castle™. $10-15.

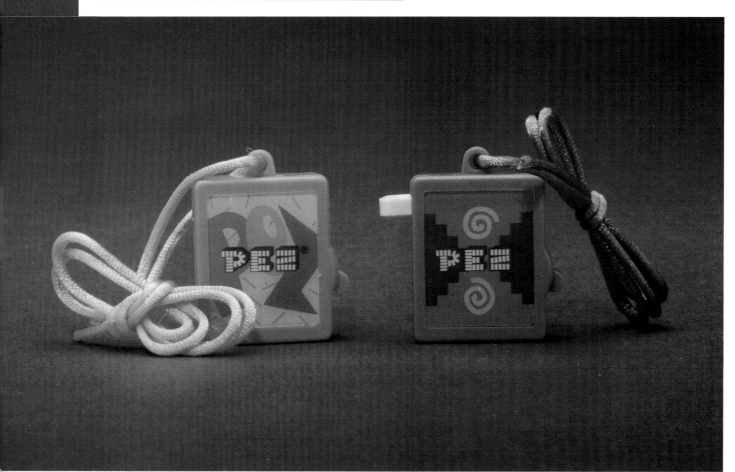

Pez® Necklace. Made by Dream Castle™. $10-15.

Pez® Bracelet. Made by Dream Castle™. $5-10.

Pez® Keychain. Made by Dream Castle™. $5-10.

Pez® Clip-on. Made by Dream Castle™. $5-10.

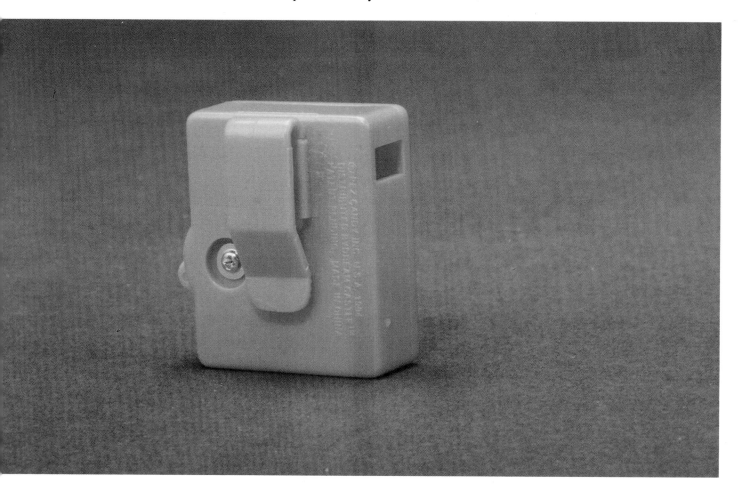

Pez® Clip-on. Back of the clip-on. Made by Dream
Castle™. $5-10.

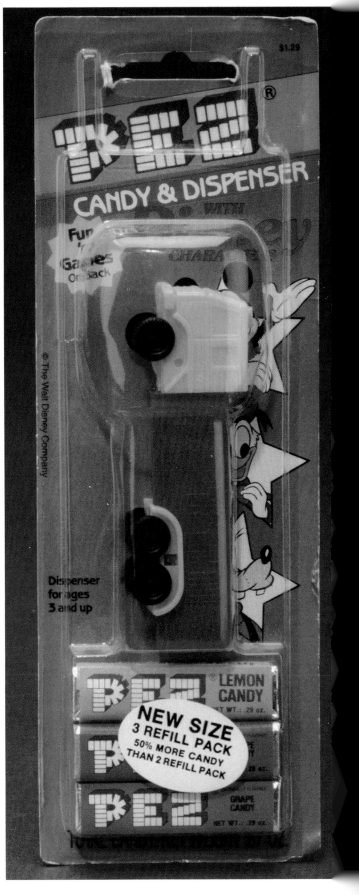

This is a blister card variation. Instead of the Disney©
card back, the dispenser is on a generic card. $2-3

These are the new series "D" trucks. The wheels are
stationary and four are available, R1, R2, R3 and R4.
Notice the wrong backing card. These are unique and
fun to look for. $1-2

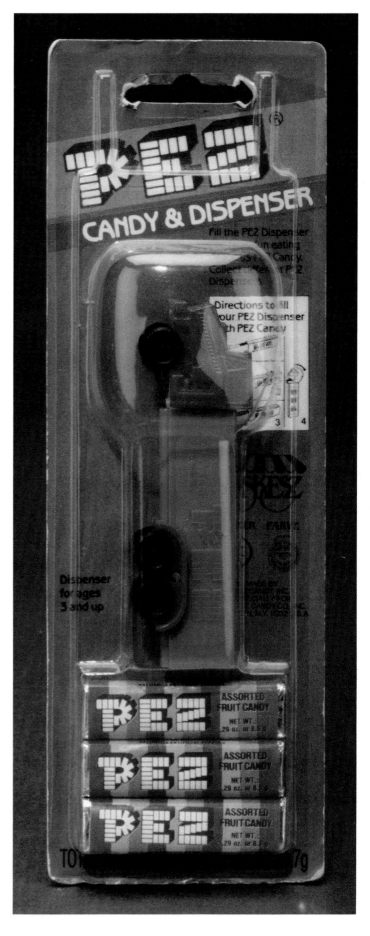

bach whistle. This dispenser comes in different color
variations. $1-2

This the new kosher Pez®. The card backing is different
from the backing used on other dispensers. $1-2

Peter Pez®. This currently available and comes with different colors for bases. $1-2

Batman©. This is on a Garfield© card backing, these are fun variations to look for and only time will tell if they will hold any value. $1-2

The correct backing for these superheros. The Batman© and Wonder Woman© dispensers are currently available. $5-10.

Hulk© dispenser, along with Spiderman©, is currently available. For some reason the Hulk© is not that easy to locate. $5-10.

Arlene©. There are five characters in this series, Nermal©
Garfield© with teeth, Garfield© with visor, Garfield©
Smiling. $1-2

Peanuts™. Dispensers available in this series, Snoopy,
Charlie, Lucy and Woodstock. $1-2

Ninja Turtle© blister card. Eight dispensers in this series. $1-2

Smurfs©. There were five characters in this series, Smurfette©, Papa Smurf©, and three Smurfs© (Red, Blue, and White Base). $10-15.

Warner Brothers© series. Daffy, Bugs Bunny, Tweety and Sylvester. $1-2

Flintstones®. Fred, Barney, Pebbles and Dino. $1-2

Valentine characters. The boy and girl Pez® Pals. $5-10.

Easter blister card. The revised Bunny, Chick in Egg, and Lamb are the characters in this series. $1-2

Halloween blister cards. The card on the right is the older blister version $5-10, the left blister is the current package, $1-2. The Witch, Skull and Revised Pumpkin are in this set.

Old Style Santa. This is another holiday blister, but the new Santa now has decal eyes, this one does not. $2-3

...ee Bear. Available in Canada and Europe during the ...olidays. Comes with or without a black strip on the ...ose. $5-10.

Canadian package. Actually rather boring with no creativity to the card. $5-10.

Merry Melody Maker. This package is available in Yugoslavia and, as you can see, it is very colorful. $5-10.

Euro-Disney®. This was available for a limited time from England. Obviously they were only available with the Disney® characters. $10-20.

Silver Glow card. This is a throw back to the old original headless dispensers, including the peppermint candy. Hungarian package. $15-20.

New revised Scrooge McDuck®. The package is boring, but it does say "Nouveau". $5-10.

European Batman©. All black Batman©, $10-20

Sugar free package. Mr. Happy Tooth package with sugar free candy. A fun and colorful card. $5-10.

Hungarian package. Very nice card with a sticker insert to make it extra colorful. $5-10.

Winter scene package. A couple variations on the packaging. This was available in Europe. $5-10

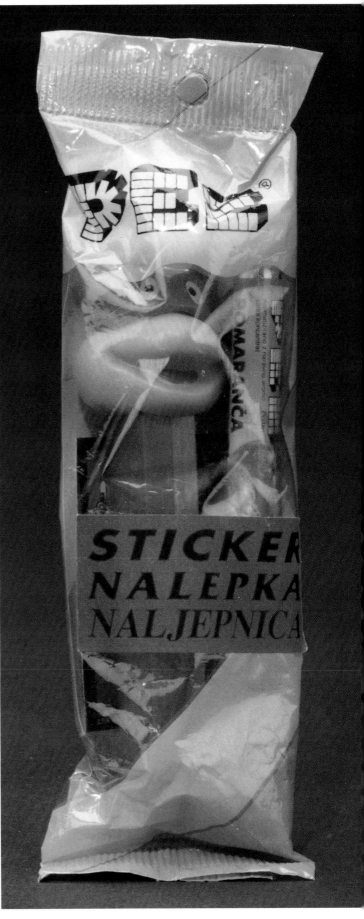

Cello bag from Yugoslavia. Enclosed is a sticker. Again, these are fun to add to your collection. $2-3

Cello bag from Yugoslavia. Sticker enclosed. $2-3

Yappy dog blister card. This is a very collectible piece.
Circa 1960's. $150-200.

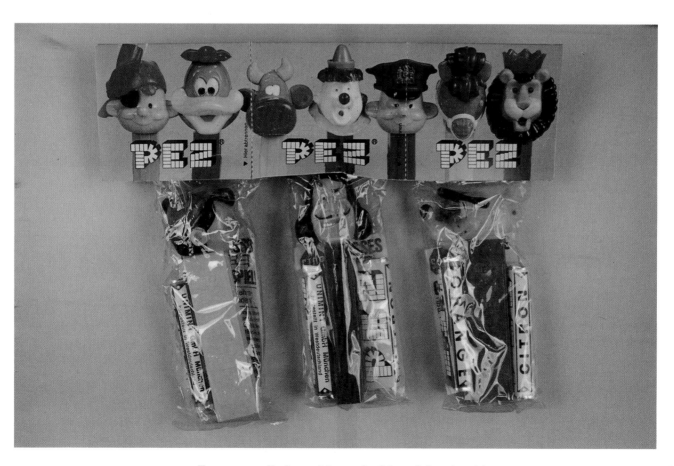

European cello bags. Very colorful, and the nice thing
about this item is that it has full color pictures of the
dispensers on the display card. Depending on the characters in the bag values can vary. $75-100.

Duck With flower blister card. Again, a very desirable piece and very difficult to find. Circa 1960's. $100-150.

Spanish Pez® E.T.™Button, E.T.™ sticker with refills. $100-150.

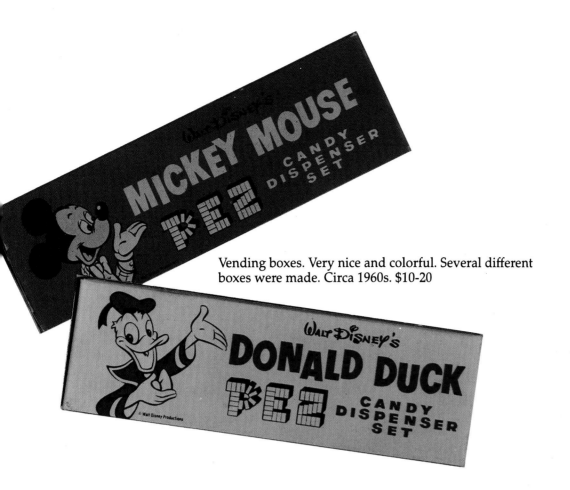

Vending boxes. Very nice and colorful. Several different boxes were made. Circa 1960s. $10-20

This is a 1931 Freight Truck Bank. Made by Ertl®. $50-75.

Pez® puzzle. This was a non-licensed item and was pulled from the market immediately. There were two different size puzzles. Made by Ceaco®. 125 pieces: $10-15; 550 pieces: $20-30.

Pez® Puzzle. This 500 piece puzzle was made for Hallmark. $10-15

Pez® Puzzle. This 500 piece puzzle is licensed and made
for Hallmark. $10-15

Chapter Two
European Accessories

Several items can be found in other countries that are not found here in the United States. This area of the hobby has proven to be very popular, although it is difficult to get an exact idea of what has been made for foreign markets and what is available. An easy way to acquire items is by asking friends who travel across the world to look out of unusual PEZ® memorabilia. Having relatives who live in different countries is also a plus.

Plastic plate. Measures 5" x 5". $20-30

Pez® plastic boats and cars. Very cheaply made. It is difficult even to see the word Pez® on the bottom of each. $5-10.

Van. HO scale, circa 1980's. $25-50.

Vending machine cards. Used inside machines to show which dispenser is available in that slot. Circa 1970s. $5-10

Vending cards. Used to identify that particular dispenser in the machine. Circa 1970's. $10-20.

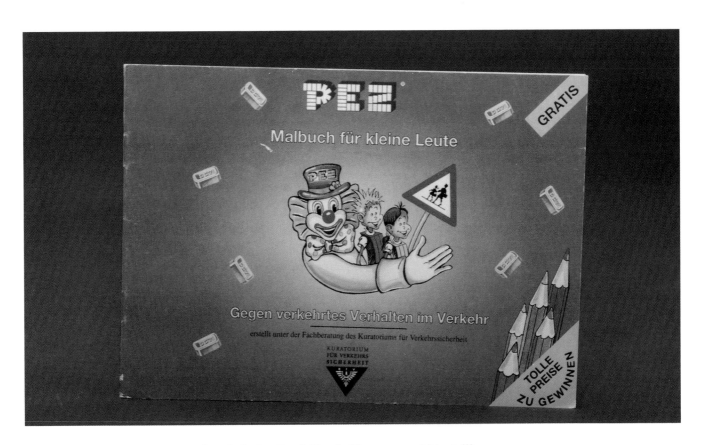

Safety Coloring Book No. 1. Given out to kids, telling
them beware of traffic safety. $5-10.

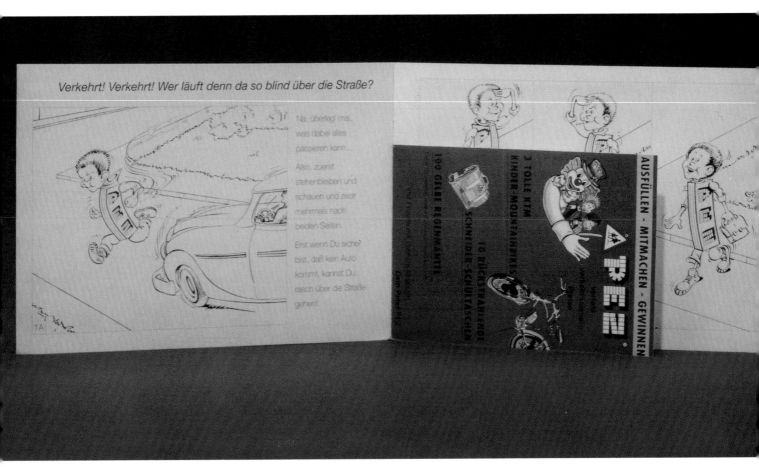

Safety Coloring Book No. 1. Insert enclosed for kids
to enter contest and win different prizes. $5-10.

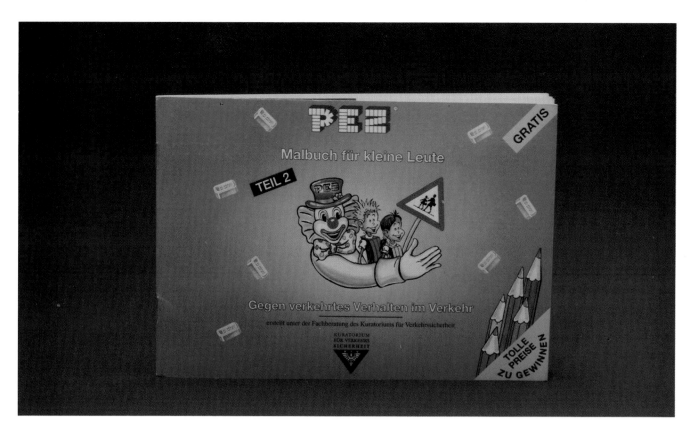

Safety Coloring Book No. 2. Given out to children to
make them aware of traffic safety. $5-10.

Safety Coloring Book No. 2. $5-10.

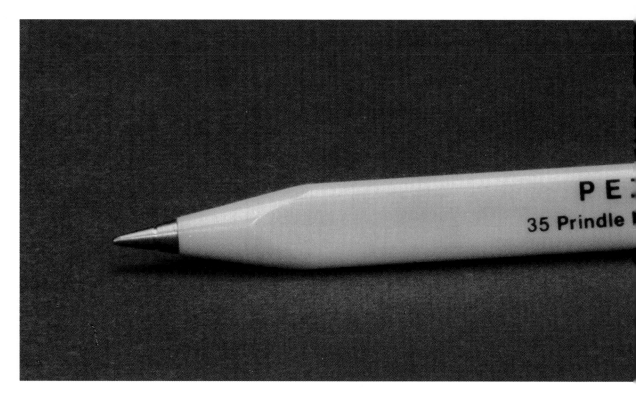

Ink pen. Given out to salesmen encouraging them to
sell Pez®. Also, given out as a premium. $50-75.

1979 Commemorative coin. Given to employees rec-
ognizing the 75 years in business. $200-250.

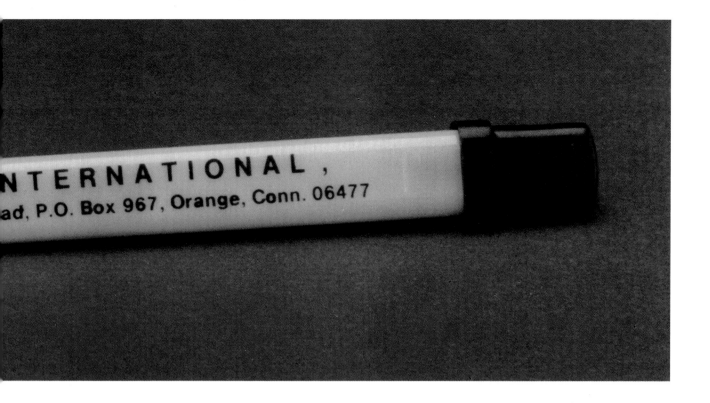

Commemorative coin, reverse. $200-250.

Knife. Given to employees, circa 1980s. $75-100.

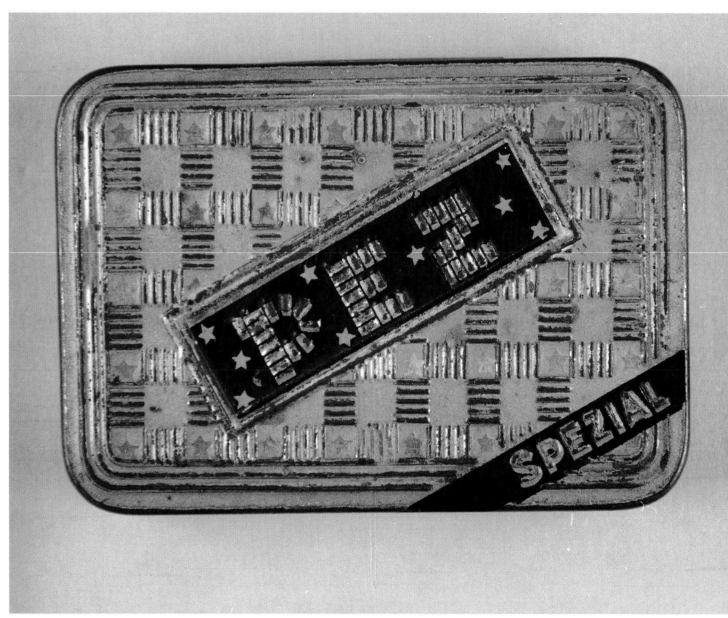

Pez® pocket tin. This item held the candy, pre-dispenser
era. Circa 1930s. $100-150

1980's Advertising poster. This is a reproduction of the 1930's advertisement, and measures 25" x 37". A classic look to early Pez®. $75-100.

1940s napkin, circa 1940s. $10-20

Promotional comic. Given out to kids. $3-5

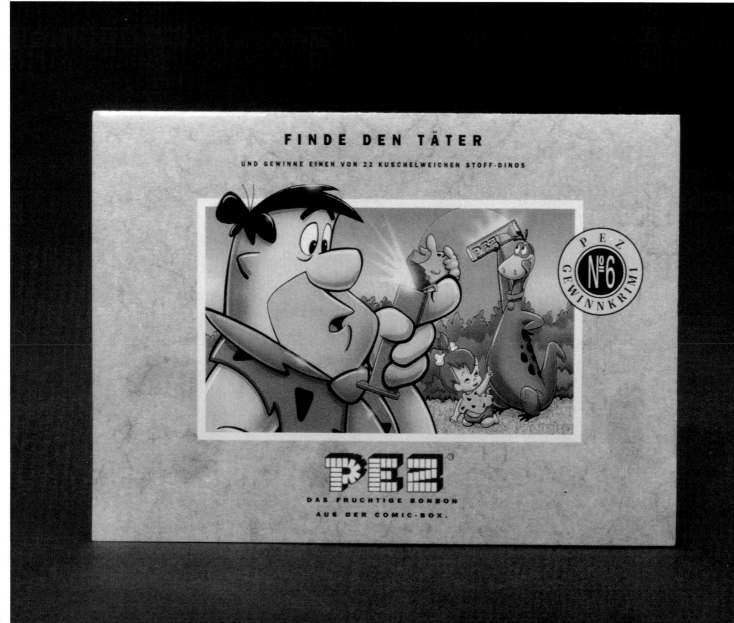

Promotional comic. $2-3

Easter boxed set. Made available in Hungary. $10-20.

Box set. Two dispensers with twelve refill packs of candy. Comes in three different colors (Pink, Yellow, and Blue). $10-20.

Box set. Two dispensers with twelve candy refills. Different characters would be available in each box. $10-20.

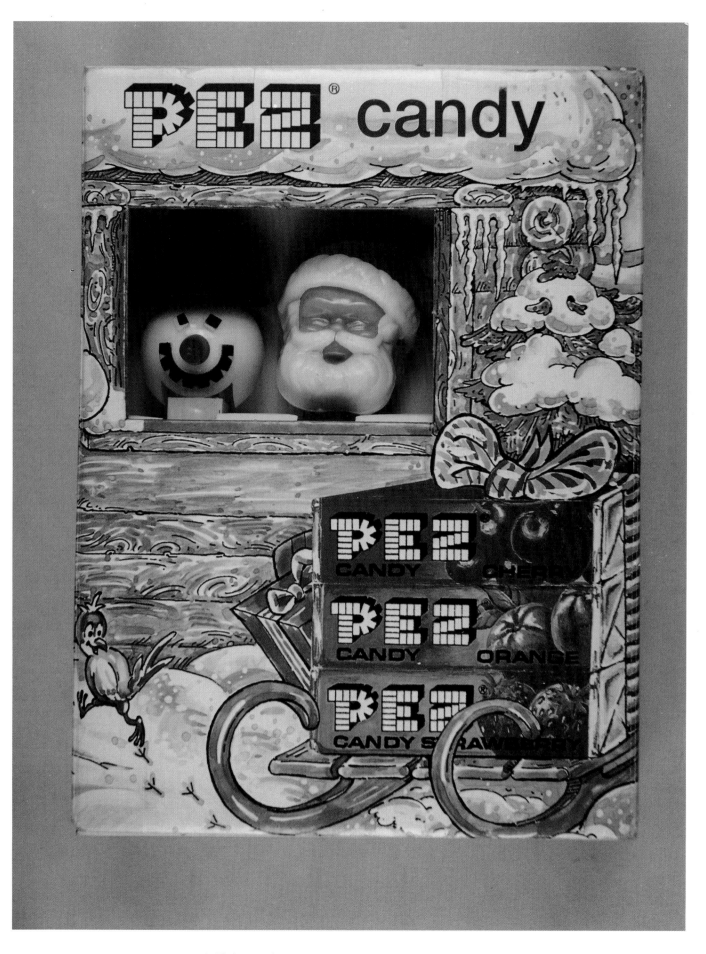

Christmas box set. Very nice scenic picture of the holiday. $10-20.

Chapter Three
Candy and Displays

Dispensers have always been the most popular area of PEZ® collecting. But a new trend has started. Today collectors are beginning to look for the candy itself. Yes, that's right, the candy is collectible. You are probably wondering if it has a bad smell to it. To tell you the truth I have some candy from the fifties and it still has the fruit fragrance to it. Collecting the boxes and the different packs of candy can make your collection that much more interesting to display. Some older packs have some very nifty premiums that one could send away for. Overall it just makes sense to have both elements together. That is what makes PEZ® so wonderful.

Easter box set. This is actually the car box but, with a Easter paper wrapping. $10-20.

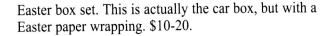

Easter box set. This is actually the car box, but with a Easter paper wrapping. $10-20.

Candy counter box. Very colorful header card. Made
in Yugoslavia. $50-75.

1950s counter refill box. Offered a space gun as a premium for just 10 wrappers and 25¢. $150-200

Chocolate candy box. Available in Hungary. $5-10

Counter box. These candies have vitamin supplements. $25-30.

Candy box of lemon flavored Pezazz. $3-5

Candy box. Featuring the Flintstones©. Hungary. $3-5

Candy counter box with plastic tray. Made in Europe.
Box $75-100, Tray $100-150

Different packs of peppermint candy. Mints $3-5, Twin-
pack $10-20, Single packs $1-3

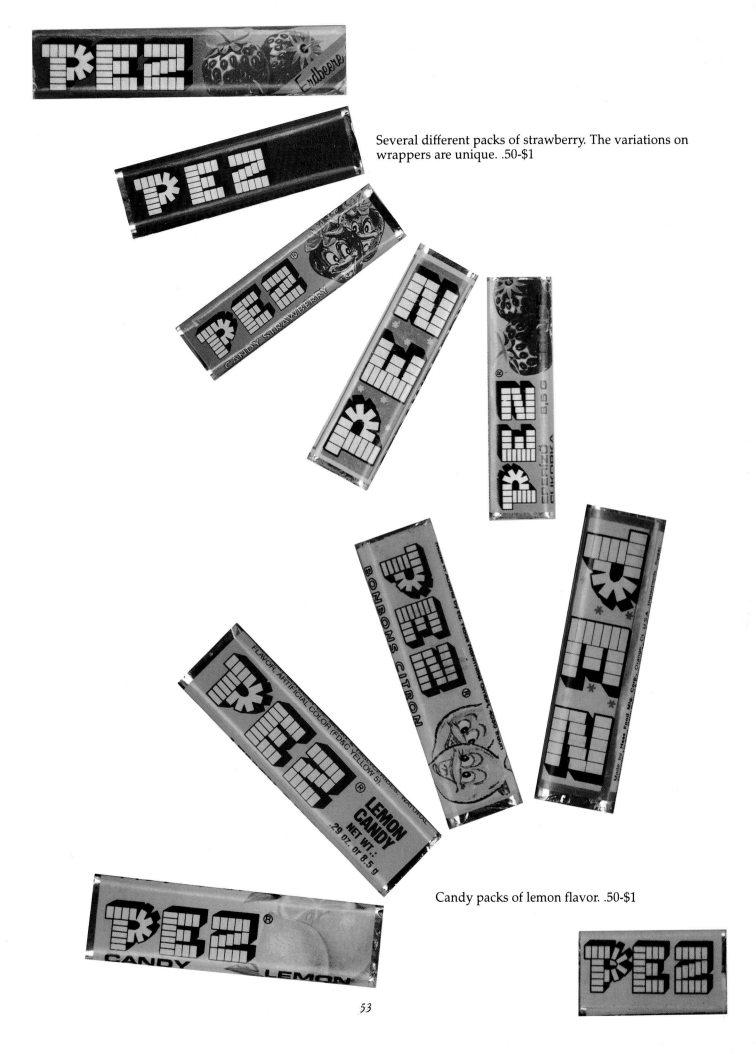

Several different packs of strawberry. The variations on wrappers are unique. .50-$1

Candy packs of lemon flavor. .50-$1

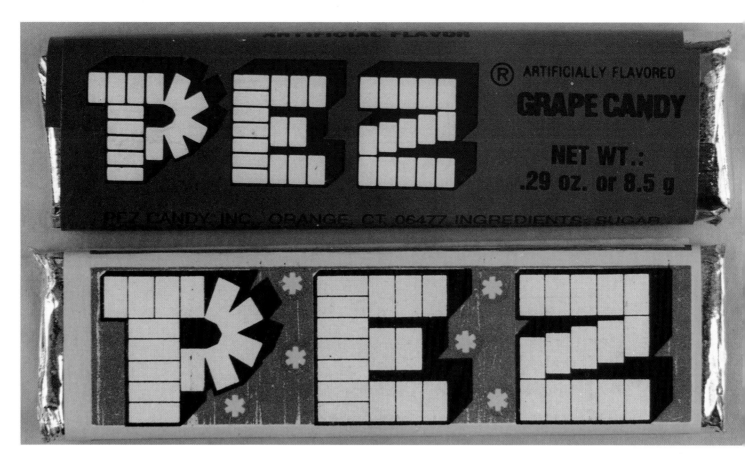

Grape single packs of candy. .50-$1

Chocolate packs. The bottom single pack is circa 1960s.
$1-5

Spanish single packs. Note: the raspberry flavor. .50-$1

Single packs of candy. Wrappers were used to send away
for the secret code flasher and personalized dispenser.
$10-20

Tick™ Comic. Issue #7. Includes Pez® in story. $2-3

Fruit gum. Hard to load in a dispenser, but fun to add to a collection. European. $1-3

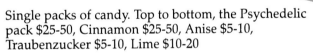

Single packs of candy. Top to bottom, the Psychedelic pack $25-50, Cinnamon $25-50, Anise $5-10, Traubenzucker $5-10, Lime $10-20

Mini packs. Made in Europe. $10-20

Chapter Four
Premiums, Inserts and Conventions

A convention was created in 1991 to bring together people whose passion for this wonderful hobby could be accepted by others who felt the same way about PEZ® dispensers. The hobby now has several meets held all around the country. It is easy enough to put together a show. Have PEZ® and people will come.

Mail-aways and freebies are another area that has become very exciting to collect and also adds that special look to anyone's collection. Most items are available very reasonable and they are fun to have and look at.

Golden Glow premium. Offered as a mail-away for wrappers. The pack of candy has a gold wrapper. Circa 1960s. Dispenser: $75-100; Candy: $20-30; Stand: $75-100. Complete set: $225-250.

Trick or Treat bag. Given out to kids at White Castle® Restaurants. The bag came with a kids meal and one halloween dispenser. Circa 1990's. $5-10.

Trick or treat bag. Given out to kids at White Castle® Restaurants. The bag came with a kids meal and one halloween dispenser. Circa 1990's. $5-10.

T-shirt. Made available as a premium in Yugoslavia.
Circa 1990s. $15-25

T-shirt offered in Europe as a mail-away. Very cheaply
made. Circa 1990s. $10-15

T-shirt offered in Europe as a mail-away. Very cheaply
made. Circa 1990s. $10-15

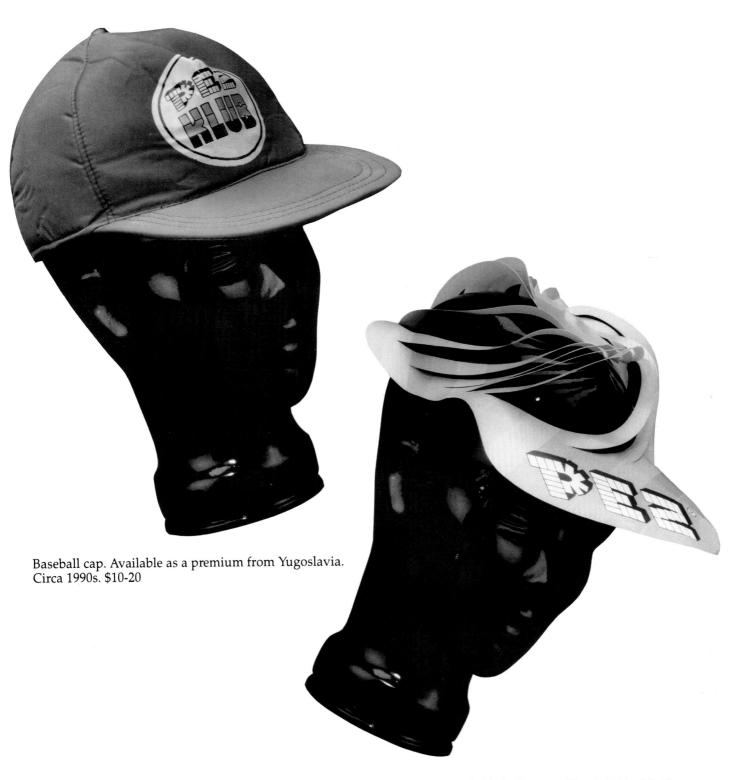

Baseball cap. Available as a premium from Yugoslavia.
Circa 1990s. $10-20

Paper visor. Available in Europe. Circa 1990's. $5-10.

Bag. This plastic bag was available in the 1970's and was given out to kids. $20-30.

Carry all double sided plastic bag. European issue. Circa 1970's. $20-30.

the Candy with a Playmate

Box-
Figuren

PEZ
aus der
PEZ-BOX

Carry all double sided plastic bag. European issue. Circa 1970's. $20-30.

Paper Hat. Enjoy wearing pictures of the Disney® superstars. Circa 1990's. $5-10.

Kids paper visor. Circa 1990's. $5-10.

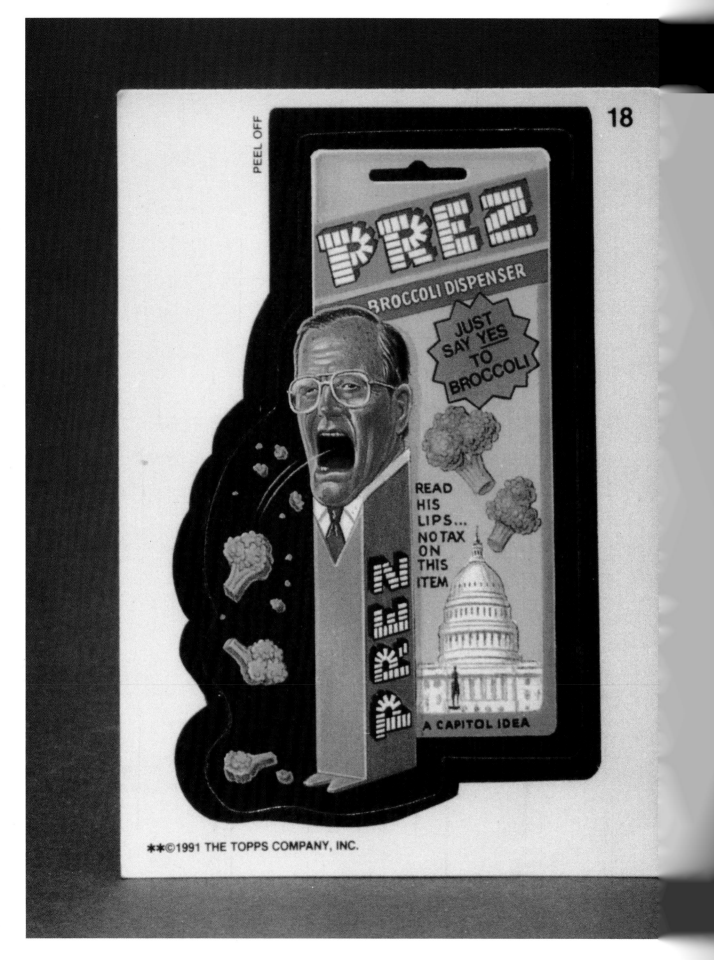

Wacky pack sticker. Circa 1990s. $1-2

Costume. Made in Spain. Circa 1990's. $5-10.

Costume, made and available in Spain. Circa 1990's. $5-10.

Costume, made in Spain. Circa 1990's. $5-10.

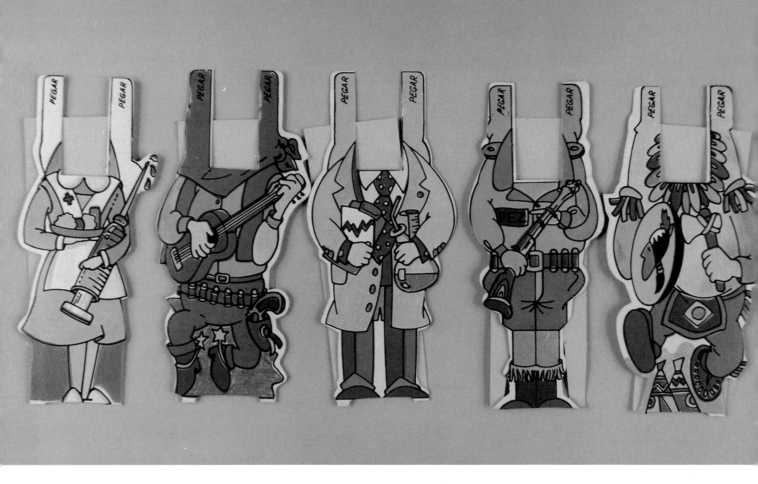

Several different costumes made in Spain. Circa 1990's.
$5-10.

Flintstone© stickers. Available in Europe, complete set of
eight. Circa 1990s. Set $10-15

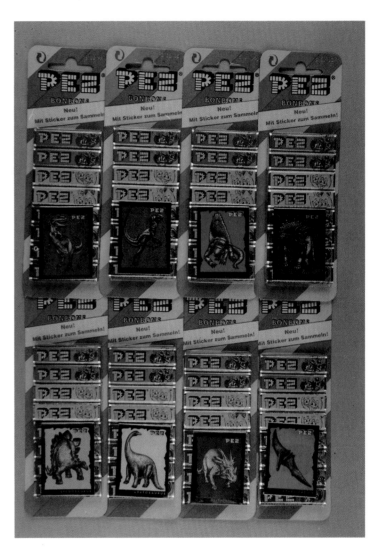

Set of eight Tom & Jerry stickers. Available in Europe. Circa 1990s. Set $10-15

Set of eight different dinosaur stickers, Available in Europe. Circa 1990s. Set $10-15

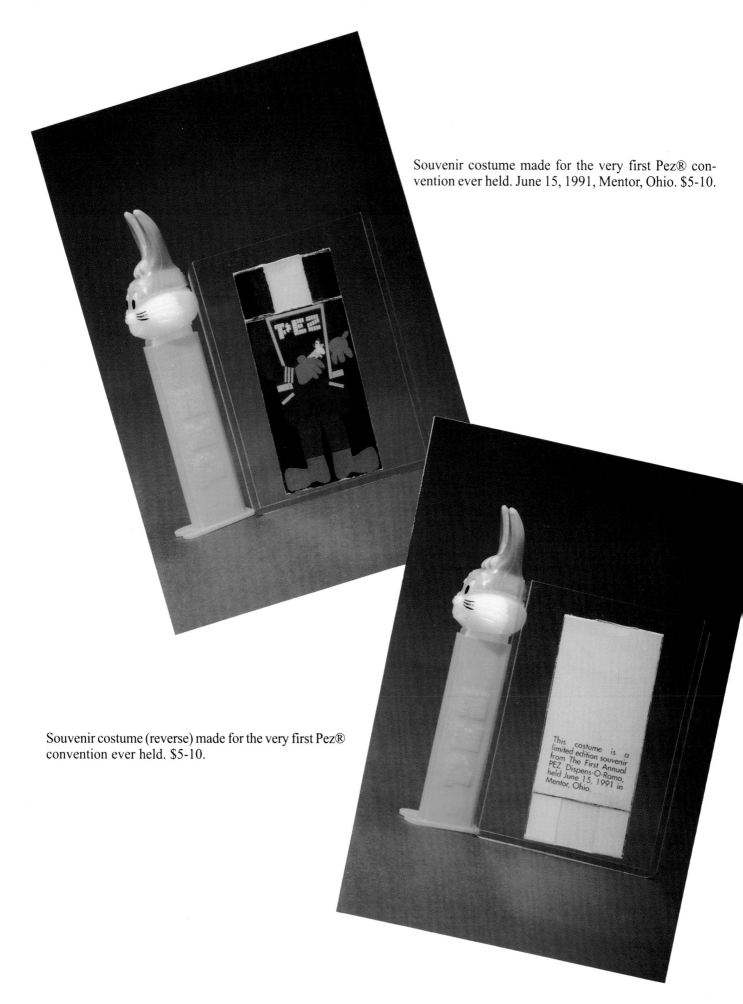

Souvenir costume made for the very first Pez® convention ever held. June 15, 1991, Mentor, Ohio. $5-10.

Souvenir costume (reverse) made for the very first Pez® convention ever held. $5-10.

This costume is a limited edition souvenir from The First Annual PEZ Dispens-O-Rama, held June 15, 1991 in Mentor, Ohio.

Convention button. Given out to registrants at the first
convention ever held. $5-10.

Button. Souvenir from the 1st convention held in Ohio.
$2-5

Souvenir button given to attendees at the first convention. $2-5

1st Convention T-shirt. Given to registrants. Held June
15, 1991, Mentor, Ohio. $15-20

Pez®-A-Mania Convention II. T-shirts given out to attendees. $15-20

Pez®-A-Mania Convention III. Souvenir T-shirts from convention held in Ohio. $8-10

Souvenir T-shirt from convention IV. Held in Ohio July
22-23 1994. $8-10

Tote bag, souvenir from Ohio convention. $3-5

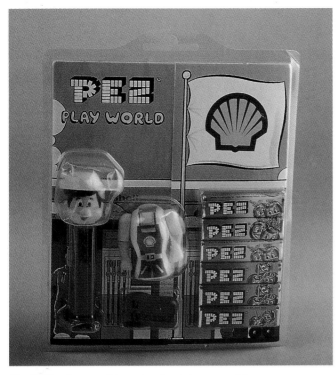

Shell Playhouse. New Pez® Pal Boy with gas attendant body parts. Available only in Europe. $20-30

Santa with body parts. Three different versions of packaging. European issue only. $10-15

Star Wars® stickers. These stickers were inserted in candy refills in Europe only. Set of 8. $10-15

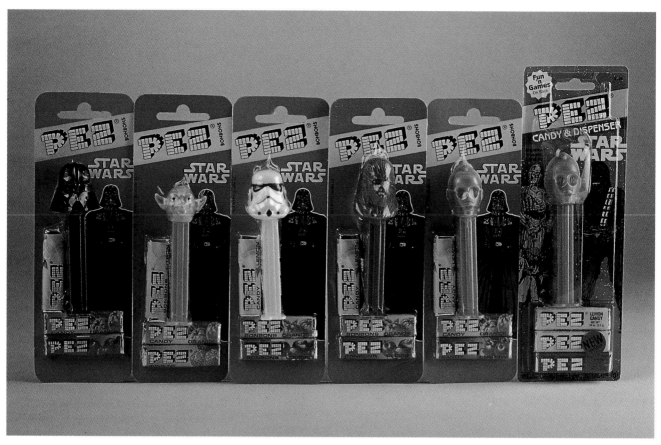

Star Wars.® Darth Vader, Yoda, Storm Trooper, Chewbacca, C3PO. American and Canadian Packaging. $3-5

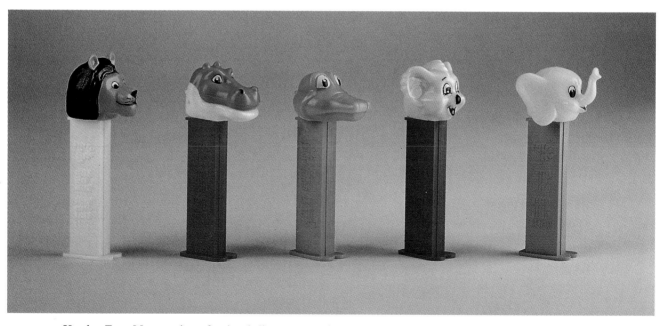

Kooky Zoo. New series of animal dispensers. Lion, hippo, alligator, koala bear, elephant. Currently available in Europe and Canada only. $1-2

Pilot, Shell and Alpine Pal, with body parts.
Available in Europe only. $10-15

Batman©. Canada and Europe are now
also using colorful packaging. $3-5

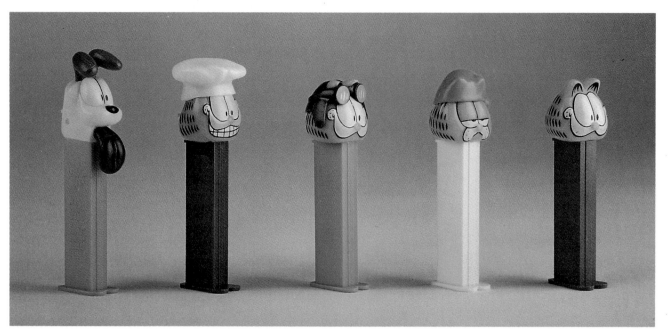

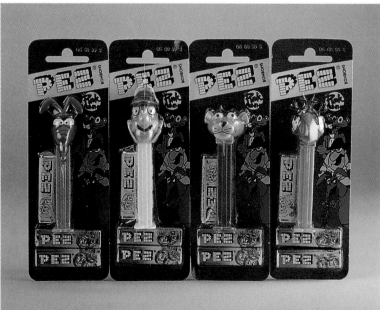

Garfield© series. Introducing Odie, along with Garfield the Baker, the Pilot, Sleepy and Regular. $1-3

Pink Panther® series. Probably the nicest and most detailed dispensers of recent issue. Anteater, Inspector, Panther, Ant. European and Canadian issue only. $3-5

European refills. Several different inserts have been included in refill packs. Stickers, tatoos and premiums. $1-3.

Notes

Notes